True Mountain Rescue Stories

Glenn Scherer

Enslow Publishers, Inc.
40 Industrial Road
Box 398
Berkeley Heights, NJ 07922
USA
http://www.enslow.com

Library of Congress Cataloging-in-Publication Data

Scherer, Glenn.

True mountain rescue stories / Glenn Scherer.

p. cm. — (True rescue stories)

Includes index.

Summary: "Read about five historic mountain rescues-from the Great Northern Railway Rescue to Beck Weathers on Mt. Everest"—Provided by publisher.

ISBN 978-0-7660-3572-0

1. Mountaineering—Search and rescue operations—Juvenile literature. 2. Mountaineering accidents—Juvenile literature. I. Title.

GV200.183.S35 2011

363.1'4—dc22 2009048202

Printed in the United States of America

082010 Lake Book Manufacturing, Inc., Melrose Park, IL

10 9 8 7 6 5 4 3 2 1

To Our Readers: We have done our best to make sure all Internet addresses in this book were active and appropriate when we went to press. However, the author and the Publisher have no control over, and assume no liability for, the material available on those Internet sites or on other Web sites they may link to. Any comments or suggestions can be sent by e-mail to comments@enslow.com or to the address on the back cover.

Enslow Publishers, Inc., is committed to printing our books on recycled paper. The paper in every book contains 10% to 30% post-consumer waste (PCW). The cover board on the outside of each book contains 100% PCW. Our goal is to do our part to help young people and the environment too!

Photo Credits: Shutterstock.com

Cover Illustration: Shutterstock.com

Contents

Mountain Facts

WORLD'S HIGHEST MOUNTAIN

Mount Everest in the Asian Himalayas straddles Nepal and Tibet. It is 29,035 feet tall (8,850 meters). As of 2007, there were 3,684 completed ascents, and 208 climbers died, a fatality rate of 5.6 percent.

WORLD'S DEADLIEST MOUNTAIN CLIMB

Annapurna, in the Himalayas, is the tenth highest peak in the world at 26,545 feet (8,091 meters). By 2007 only 153 people had conquered Annapurna, but 61 climbers had died there, a fatality rate of 39 percent.

OTHER DEADLY ASCENTS

Nanga Parbat, Earth's ninth highest peak at 26,660 feet (8,125 meters), has been summited by 287 climbers, but 64 climbers have died, a fatality rate of 28 percent. Another dangerous peak is K2, the second highest mountain in the world, at 28,250 feet (8,611 meters). With 302 successful climbs and 77 fatalities, it has a 25 percent fatality rate.

UNITED STATES' HIGHEST MOUNTAIN

Denali (Mt. McKinley) in Alaska is 20,320 feet tall (6,193 meters). It has claimed nearly one hundred lives, though with thousands of climbers annually, the fatality rate is relatively low.

U.S. EAST'S DEADLIEST MOUNTAIN

Mount Washington in New Hampshire is only 6,288 feet (1,916 meters) tall. But its location—where three storm tracks meet—produces horrific winds and weather. One of the highest wind gusts ever (231 miles per hour), was recorded on Mt. Washington. More than a hundred climbers have died there. Small crosses mark the spots where they lost their lives.

U.S. WEST'S DEADLIEST MOUNTAIN

Oregon's Mount Hood, 11,239 feet tall (3,426 meters), is the second most climbed mountain in the world. About 10,000 climbers a year try the ascent, and 130 have died since record keeping began over a hundred years ago.

WORST U.S. AVALANCHE DISASTER

The 1910 Great Northern Railway avalanche in Washington State's Cascade Mountains was the deadliest in the nation, killing at least ninety-six people.

THE TWO DEADLIEST AVALANCHES IN HISTORY

On January 10, 1962, an avalanche in Ranrahirca, in the Peruvian Andes, killed 4,000 people. On May 30, 1970, a bigger avalanche happened in the same place. An earthquake triggered the release of a massive wall of ice on Mount Huascaran, 22,205 feet tall (6,768 meters). Within three minutes the avalanche slid 6 miles (10 kilometers) down a glacier, destroying Ranrahirca and the town of Yungay. About 20,000 people died, with just 400 survivors.

Chapter 1

Avalanche! The Great Northern Railway Rescue

By 1910 it must have seemed to most people that machines had beaten nature. The Wright brothers' plane had conquered the skies. Barney Oldfield's racecar was about to top speeds of 130 miles per hour. And trips that took months by covered wagon could be made in just days by railroad.

Unfortunately, the nation's railway builders took some big risks to conquer the Western mountains. Their trains often climbed over high alpine passes. The tracks ran along cliffs where the risk of snow slides was high.

Trapped in the Mountains

Still, no one guessed what lay ahead when two Great Northern Railway trains headed for the Pacific Coast on February 23, 1910. About 125 passengers and crew chugged east on Spokane Local Passenger Train No. 25 and Fast Mail Train No. 27.

All went well until the trains entered the Cascade Mountains. On the east side of the Cascade Tunnel, a blizzard closed the tracks completely. Both trains were stopped at the little railroad town of Wellington, Washington. There they sat on the edge of a steep ravine beneath Windy Mountain.

At first, no one worried, but the delay grew longer and longer. The powerful steam-driven rotary snowplows that normally kept the tracks clear were no match for the fierce winter snows.

The bored passengers and crew played cards and read books. They wrote letters that they couldn't mail. They trudged each day to the local hotel to eat their meals. Still the snow fell. The trains were slowly buried under the drifts. Some passengers began to worry about the chance of an avalanche, also called a "snow slide."

The avalanche risk was greatened by the fact that Windy Mountain had recently been logged and burned by forest fires. That meant fewer trees to hold the snow in place.

On February 26, the blizzard knocked down the

telegraph wires. Now the trains and the town of Wellington were cut off from the outside world.

The Snows Run Red with Blood

Then the weather warmed. The snowstorm that had kept the trains trapped almost a week now turned to rain. There was fierce thunder and lightning. Still, few guessed at the danger they were in.

Then on the night of March 1, at 1:42 A.M., the weight of the rain finally caused the huge drifts of snow that hung above the trains to let loose. An avalanche raged down the side of Windy Mountain.

"It seemed as if the world were coming to an end," said one Wellington townsperson. "I saw the whole side of the mountain coming down, tearing up everything in its way."

The avalanche carried all in its path, including snow, ice, trees, and rocks. In seconds both trains were engulfed. They were knocked off the tracks and into the ravine. The train engines tumbled down the slope. The wooden passenger cars flew through the air. They splintered and came apart like shattering eggshells. Metal and wooden fragments impaled people and cut them to pieces. People shrieked in pain and confusion as they fell through the darkness.

Passengers and crew fell all the way to Tye Creek, deep in the ravine. Some were buried under 40 feet of snow. Their bodies wouldn't be found until spring.

Townspeople to the Rescue

There were roughly 125 people sleeping on the trains that night. To the railroad workers who lived in Wellington, it seemed certain that all of those people were dead.

Still, the townspeople came out into the driving rain and darkness to help. Some, without thinking of their own safety, began climbing down the ravine to offer any aid they could to anyone lucky enough to have survived.

Amazingly, some passengers and crew were still alive. Some buried amid the snow and wreckage "swam" up through the drifts and darkness to save themselves. On the mail train, a buried conductor dug himself out. Then, in a flash of lightning, he saw a hand sticking out of the snow. Digging in a hurry, the conductor was able to free another crewman from his tomb of snow.

Two Wellington men, Charles Andrews and Bob Miles, went down into the canyon. They found a man and woman still alive, buried up to their necks in snow. The two men dug with bare hands to free the couple. But the snow was packed as tight as stone. The men ran to get shovels, but when they returned, they found the couple dead.

One rescuer, William Flannery, found an injured passenger. He lifted the hurt man onto his back. But a new avalanche hit both of them. Flannery himself was buried in snow, dug himself out, and then stumbled into Tye Creek. Unable to find the man he had been trying to save, Flannery instead helped rescue Duncan Tegtmeier, the engineer of one of the doomed trains.

A seven-year-old boy, Raymond Starrett, was found with a jagged 30-inch wooden fragment stuck in his forehead. A rescuer—not a doctor—operated on the boy, removing the inch-wide splinter with a shaving razor. Amazingly, the child lived.

Perhaps the most astounding rescue of all was of an eighteen-month-old infant. The baby, named Varden Gray, survived the night buried in snow. Not only did Varden live; so did his parents, even though they had been buried all night nearby.

By the time dawn came on March 1, the rescuers began to lose hope. There were no more cries for help. Anyone entombed was assumed dead.

Then, eleven hours after the avalanche, Charles

Andrews heard "a mewing far off, like a kitten." The rescuers rushed to the sound and dug. Within minutes they uncovered a final survivor. It was Ida Starrett, mother of the boy Ray Starrett, who had been found alive with the splinter in his head. Mother and child were reunited, though other members of their family were lost, according to Gary Krist in his thrilling book about the disaster called *The White Cascade*.

Aftermath

The townspeople, cut off from the outside world, set up a crude hospital. They gave the survivors first aid, and fed and warmed them. Though at least ninety-six people died that night (maybe more), twenty-three were saved.

Days later, when the tracks had been cleared and help arrived, rescued train engineer Duncan Tegtmeier was asked by a reporter what he would do when he was able to walk again. "Why, get them to give me another engine, of course," said Tegtmeier. "Do you think I am going to waste five years I spent learning this trade just because I got in this one bad shakeup!"

In 1929 a new tunnel was built beneath Windy Mountain, replacing the old track. The abandoned rail bed and site of the disaster can still be walked today.

Avalanche Safety

Snow slides are deadly: Only one in three people buried by an avalanche survives. The best tip for surviving is to avoid getting caught in an avalanche. Here's how:

- **Be aware:**
  Mountain travel on snow requires avalanche readiness. Never travel alone. If you think conditions are unsafe, change your travel plans.
- **Learn to read the land:**
  Avoid climbing steep, unstable slopes unless you have the right gear, are with an experienced climber, and have had mountaineer training.
- **Watch for bad weather:**
  Storms cause most avalanches. But long periods of cold, clear weather can also weaken snow and trigger a slide.
- **Obey signs**
  If you see an avalanche warning, find somewhere else to engage in your activity. Check with rangers before climbing. Also check the Web site of the Avalanche Network (found in the back of this book) for warnings.
- **If caught in an avalanche:**
  Never try to outrun a snow slide. Try to ride it down, staying atop the snow on your belly with head facing downhill, steering with your hands.

It is now the Iron Goat Trail. This hiking path takes walkers to the site of the deadliest avalanche in U.S. history, and to the ghost town of Wellington, now all but forgotten.

Chapter 2

Survival Against All Odds: Crash on Camel's Hump

Each year thousands of hikers climb Camel's Hump Mountain in Vermont. They pass the aging wreck of a B-24 bomber. The plane's right wing lies upside down along the Alpine Trail, just below the peak's granite summit. This wreckage hints at an amazing tale of survival and rescue that unfolded more than sixty years ago.

Fateful Meeting with a Mountain

It was Sunday, October, 15, 1944. World War II was at its height. Millions of soldiers were battling and dying around the world.

The ten-man crew of a B-24 Liberator bomber stationed in Massachusetts had not yet seen combat. That day, at about 11:00 P.M. they took off on a routine training mission to Vermont.

As part of the men's training, they were flying

blind. Their cockpit windshield was covered with canvas. The airmen were ordered to complete their flight using only instruments, including maps and a compass.

Pilot David Potter took the plane to an altitude of 8,000 feet (2,438 meters). That put it safely above all of New England's mountain peaks. However, at that height the temperature was only about 6°F. Though the plane was equipped to supply electricity to heated flight suits, the crew didn't have such snug outfits. Instead, they wore just their fleece-lined jackets. They shivered in the cold.

The pilot, maybe to warm his crew, took the plane down to 4,000 feet (1,219 meters). There the air was warmer. Though most Vermont mountain peaks still weren't high enough to be a threat to the plane, one now stood directly in the way. At 4,083 feet (1,244 meters), Camel's Hump is one of the state's highest summits.

The 36,000-pound bomber smashed into the southeast summit of Camel's Hump at 215 miles (346 kilometers) per hour. The plane was ripped to pieces as it struck the trees and granite slopes. The remains of the bomber came to a halt in freshly fallen snow.

Most of the crew was killed on impact. But one

man remained alive. That was eighteen-year-old gunner Private James William Wilson. It was 1:58 A.M., on Monday, October 16, 1944.

Saving Private Wilson

The temperature on Camel's Hump that night was in the low twenties Fahrenheit. Wilson was barely conscious inside the plane's broken fuselage, unable to move. He couldn't protect himself from the cold. Worse, no one knew what had happened to the bomber.

When the plane didn't return by three o'clock in the morning, a search began. But by dawn clouds moved in, hiding the wreck from search aircraft. As the hours of that cold Monday drifted by, Wilson lay atop Camel's Hump exposed to the dangers of frostbite.

On Tuesday afternoon the clouds lifted and an Army search plane spotted the wreck. Unfortunately, the position given for the crash site was wrong. That delayed a ground search for the plane.

Finally a search party gathered in the small nearby town of Waterbury, Vermont. Civil Air Patrol Major William Mason organized it. His group was mostly made up of young Civil Air Patrol cadets from

Waterbury High School. The teenage cadets had two other guides with them. They were Dr. Edwin Steele, an expert woodsman and hiker, and Clair Lewis, who knew the mountain well.

The rescuers drove to the base of Camel's Hump in a pickup truck and began climbing to the southeast side of the summit.

At the top, the search party spotted the wreck with the help of a circling U.S. Army plane. Mason, Steele, and five of the high school teens descended about one hundred feet to the wreck, while the rest of the rescuers returned to Waterbury for more help. The ripped and scattered remains of engines, wings, fuselage, broken trees, and mangled corpses made the group sure no one could have survived. Then they heard a faint voice.

It was Private Wilson. He was still alive. He had spent forty-one hours—two subfreezing nights—on the mountain. It was 7:15 P.M. on Tuesday, and night was falling.

The Cadets Take Action

Dr. Steele found that Wilson had a badly broken knee. Mason, Steele, and the cadets wrapped Wilson in parachutes. They built a small lean-to, a crude shelter, around him and lit a fire.

Still, Airman Wilson was in rough shape. He was unable to say his name and was very confused. His rescuers worried that the flyer wouldn't survive the night. Two official U.S. Army rescue teams arrived the next day, Wednesday.

Some local men tied Wilson to a stretcher and got ready to take him down the mountain. Others looked for more survivors. But no one else had lived through the crash. The searchers gathered the dead. They prepared to bring them down the mountain for burial.

By mistake the rescuers failed to descend by one of the easier trails. Instead, they came down Camel's Hump on the Long Trail. This is one of the most difficult hiking trails in the eastern United States. It is known for its steep cliffs and boulders. Wilson, now awake, talked with his rescuers. He urged them not to drop him.

At the bottom of the mountain, U.S. Army men informed the local townspeople that the military would take over the stretcher from there. But the local folk, who had carried Wilson safely down from the peak, refused. They proudly carried Wilson past the local reporters who had gathered in an attempt to get the story of the rescue.

In the next few days, nine coffins holding the remains of the dead airmen were sent to their hometowns for burial. Unfortunately, the bodies had been so mutilated that it was hard to recognize the flyers. In truth, one dead crewman had been left behind on Camel's Hump. He wouldn't be found and buried until the following spring.

A Long Recovery, a Meaningful Life

For Jim Wilson a long, brave road to recovery lay ahead. His two cold nights on Camel's Hump left him with frostbitten hands and feet. Unfortunately, gangrene had set in on his frozen limbs. Gangrene is the death of body tissue, which results in deadly infection.

To save Wilson's life, both arms had to be removed below the elbow, and both legs below the knee. Wilson was the first U.S. soldier to undergo such extreme surgery in World War II. The operation left Wilson in shock. He also got double pneumonia and lost 70 pounds (31.7 kilograms). He was very depressed.

To help with Wilson's despair, doctors put him in a ward with other amputees. The patients kidded and joked with him. Wilson was soon given a set of hooks for hands. Though he dumped his first tray of food on himself, he quickly learned to use them. Next, he was fitted with artificial legs. Soon he was climbing up and down a training staircase. He was released from the hospital in 1946.

In 1948, Wilson drove a car to Vermont to meet and thank Steele, Mason, the cadets, and other rescuers. He went on to graduate from college with a law degree and got married. He settled in Colorado but traveled the country visiting veterans' hospitals. There he urged other amputees to have hope and live full lives.

He also pushed for better laws to protect disabled people. He even met with U.S. President Harry Truman to argue for people's disability rights. He continued to practice law for decades.

"Jimmy marched on through life as if it were nothing for him not to have hands or feet," said Vermont historian Brian Lindner, who wrote a book about the bomber crash. "One of his last comments to me was 'You know, I survived that plane crash, but cigarette smoking is killing me.'" Jim Wilson died at Christmas 2001 of emphysema, brought on by smoking.

"He has done more and better things with his life since the [1944 bomber] crash than most people would

Heading off Hypothermia

Hypothermia is low body temperature caused by exposure to cold or wet conditions. It is the most common threat to winter travelers, but can happen when temperatures are well above freezing. Victims become confused, lose their way, and even fight their rescuers. Untreated hypothermia kills. Here's how to prevent it:

- **Plan an escape route:**
  Know safe shortcuts for bailing out of an outdoor activity.

- **Drink lots of water even in winter:**
  A well-hydrated body is resistant to hypothermia.

- **Get a weather forecast:**
  Know what the weather will be where you will be traveling. Remember that the higher you go on a mountain, the colder, windier, and stormier it gets.

- **Dress for the weather:**
  Wear layered clothing that will keep you warm and dry. Avoid cotton clothing (such as T-shirts) because cotton soaks up water. Always carry a raincoat and extra clothes, even when the weather report says warm and sunny.

- **Know the symptoms:**
  If you feel cold, shiver, feel tired, confused, or clumsy, you could have hypothermia. Stop climbing. Get warm. Keep moving. Seek shelter or build a fire.

accomplish in a life without the burden of artificial limbs," wrote Lindner in his book.

The 1944 crash led to the placing of a warning beacon near Camel's Hump and to the founding of a mountain rescue team in central Vermont. The B-24 wreck on the peak still attracts the curious.

Chapter 3

The Rescuers Become the Rescued: Chopper Crash

After the 1950s, mountaineering grew to become a multibillion-dollar business. Today, thousands of climbers scale the world's peaks each year. Meanwhile, a second activity has grown up around mountaineering. That activity is mountain search and rescue.

In the world's alpine regions, military and civilian rescue teams risk their lives to save climbers in trouble. Some are paid to do it. Others volunteer. Their equipment includes helicopters that fly in bad weather and up to dangerous altitudes. Sadly, sometimes the rescuers also get into trouble. Then the rescuers become the rescued.

One such event took place on Oregon's Mount Hood in 2002. Mount Hood's snow-covered peak rises to 11,239 feet (3,426 meters). This dormant volcano is far from being one of the world's highest mountains. But it is the second most climbed peak on Earth, after Japan's Mount Fuji.

Mount Hood attracts ten thousand climbers each year. They try to reach its peak in a four- to eight-hour climb. While most get down safely, 130 people have died in climbing accidents on the mountain since 1896.

A Perfect Day for Climbing

May 30, 2002, dawned as a beautiful, blue-sky day on Mount Hood. The good weather drew lots of climbers. As it turned out, the large crowd would make the peak very unsafe that day.

Many Mount Hood climbers start their ascent before dawn. They reach the top by midmorning, then go down before dark. This day, several climbing groups reached the summit at the same early hour. Then they started down together. To someone watching from far below, all of those climbers in their bright parkas spread out on their climbing ropes must have looked like colorful beads on strings.

The climbing groups were about 800 feet (244 meters) below Mount Hood's summit at around nine o'clock in the morning. Suddenly someone slipped on the ice.

As this first climber fell, he jerked three other roped climbers after him. The climbers on the rope tried to self-arrest; that is, they each rolled onto their stomachs and slammed their ice axes into the snow. But the slushy snow did not hold.

The four men tumbled in free fall. They hit two more climbers on another rope below them. They then plowed into three more climbers on another rope.

All together, nine climbers were torn free from the mountain. All plunged into a 20-foot deep crevasse at 10,700 feet altitude. Three of the climbers died. Four were injured. Two were unhurt.

Choppers to the Rescue

Nearby climbers quickly went to work to help pull their fellow mountaineers out of the crevasse. They offered first aid using the supplies they carried.

Another climber made a cell phone call to the local mountain rescue team. Soon rescue helicopters were throbbing up toward the top of Mount Hood.

At first the rescue went well. The chopper teams airlifted the two most hurt climbers off the mountain and to a local hospital.

Then, at 1:52 P.M., a helicopter from the Air Force's 304th Rescue Squadron flew in to save the third injured climber. The chopper suddenly lost lift and crashed onto the mountain. Luckily, an alert crewman released a cable hooked to the stretcher in which the injured climber lay. This stopped the injured climber from being dragged after the crashing chopper.

The five would-be rescuers on the helicopter were lucky, too. Only one was hurt. None were killed. This is amazing, considering the chopper rolled over on top of one of the helicopter rescue team members.

Two TV station helicopters caught the crash on videotape. This footage was later shown around the world.

Rescuing the Rescuers

The rescue mission leader, Steve Rollins of Portland Mountain Rescue, took charge.

"As the incident commander, I had to take a step back." said Rollins later. "I had to look at the whole situation," [and ask myself:] "Is the [crashed] helicopter going to blow up? We are right in an avalanche and icefall path. Does that matter? Does it make more sense to keep these guys [where they are] or, like combat rescue, do we pick them up and drag them to a safe location, then assess [their injuries]?"

Rollins made safe choices that protected the injured climbers and the helicopter crew. His quick, clear thinking made sure that no one else died on Mount Hood that day.

Two more helicopters were rushed in to take the place of the chopper that crashed. These choppers took out two more injured climbers. The injured helicopter rescue team was skied off the mountain or taken down by chopper.

By 4:30 P.M. all the survivors had been rescued. Now the rescue teams had the task of recovering the three bodies of the climbers that fell into the crevasse.

A Climbing Controversy

News reports about the combined climbing and helicopter accidents raised questions about mountain safety. People asked whether mountaineers taking part in the thrill sport of climbing had a right to put the rescuers' lives at risk.

Steve Rollins brushed these questions aside. "The key thing to understand is that no one forces search and rescue team members to rescue climbers. Just as

Safe Mountain Travel

The trouble on Mount Hood started when too many climbers were clustered too close together on slippery ice. Here are some tips for safe climbing:

- **Get trained:**
  Never climb without getting properly trained in mountaineering skills.

- **Have the proper gear:**
  Never do technical climbing without the right equipment (ropes, harness,, ice ax, etc.).

- **Know your limits:**
  Never push past your physical limits. Conserve enough energy to get up the mountain and enough to get back down.

- **Turn back if there is trouble:**
  Never keep pushing on if there is a problem. Return the way you came or take a safe shortcut down.

- **Buddy up:**
  Travel with a companion or several companions.

- **Don't follow too close:**
  Keep a safe distance between climbers.

- **Pay attention to conditions:**
  At any sign of bad weather, turn around and go down.

the climbers know and accept the risks of their climb, rescuers know and accept the risks of the rescue. We choose to do it; we accept responsibility for our own actions. For me mountain rescue is as much a sport as mountaineering is. And it's rewarding to be able to help someone out."

In recent years, mountain search and rescue teams have become a vital part of the mountaineering scene. The bravery and self-sacrifice of these rescuers have helped save many lives. But search and rescue expert Rollins warns, "Some people think rescue work is glamorous. We discourage these people from joining the rescue team. In reality, most rescue work is very hard, in difficult and relatively dangerous conditions."

Chapter 4

Crawling Down a Mountain: Joe Simpson in the Andes

Mountaineers have a saying: "There are old climbers, and there are bold climbers, but there are no old, bold climbers." Joe Simpson is an exception to that rule. He is certainly a bold mountain climber. But good luck, great courage, and strength have got him through some very close scrapes with death.

Take for example his 2,000-foot (609-meter) fall in an avalanche in the French Alps without a helmet. He lived to climb another day.

Another close call occurred when Simpson was climbing again in the Alps with Ian Whittaker in 1984. A ledge dropped away from beneath the two climbers just moments after they had secured themselves to a rock face with climbing pitons. That left them bootless, dangling helpless in their sleeping bags high above a glacier. More than twelve hours later, a rescue team dropped in from above by helicopter. The rescuers used a winch to save the two climbers.

But this seems like nothing when compared with what happened to Joe Simpson and his climbing partner Simon Yates in June 1985. That's when they trekked into a remote part of Peru. Their goal was to ascend to the more than 20,000-foot (6,096-meter) summit of Siula Grande peak. They would climb up the west face, one of the highest unclimbed mountain routes in South America.

The result was one of the great "self-rescues" in all of mountaineering history. When the two climbers got in trouble, they were far from help. They had no one to rely on but themselves.

To the Summit

Simpson and Yates climbed using the "Alpine style." This meant that they climbed quickly, without a series of base camps equipped with supplies. Instead, they set up a single base camp at 14,764 feet altitude (4,500 meters). What this also meant was that if something went wrong, they had little room for error.

Driven down by bad weather on their first attempt, they started climbing a second time on June 4, 1985.

The climb was hard, and took three-and-a-half days. The men picked their way up steep ice slopes at an eighty-degree angle. They crossed unstable ice and snow sheets, which threatened to give way beneath their feet. There was a constant risk of avalanche.

Tired, they reached the top on June 7. They stayed for just thirty minutes. It was already late, two thirty in the afternoon, when they began their descent. Almost at once they were closed in and slowed by clouds and snow.

Disaster

The two friends made their way down along very dangerous, knife-edge ridges. Suddenly an ice ledge broke away, and Joe Simpson fell 20 feet (6 meters). Simon Yates descended to find Joe with a badly broken right leg.

Simon's first thought was that Joe would die on the mountain. There were no helicopters, no alpine huts, no series of supply tents, and no other climbers or rescue teams to call for help. At that altitude the broken leg was like a death sentence.

Still, the two climbers decided to try to get down to safety and back to their base camp. This is how they did it: Simon dug out a seat in the snow. He planted himself there. Then he slowly let out rope, lowering Joe down the mountain. Joe, in terrible pain, slid along until he reached the end of the rope. This is called belaying. Next Simon would belay down to Joe. Then the two men would repeat the process.

Everything went well until Joe was out of sight of Simon, and was lowered over an ice cliff. There Joe dangled, with frostbitten hands. He was unable to climb back up.

Simon didn't have the strength to pull Joe back up either. Worse, over the next hour Simon slowly lost his position as his snow seat began to collapse.

If he didn't act quickly, Simon would be dragged along after Joe. Both would fall to their deaths. Simon had only one choice. He did what mountain climbers are never supposed to do. He cut the rope connecting the two mountaineers and friends together. He saved himself, but it was likely that he killed Joe.

Into the Abyss

Joe fell through the darkness of night, at the end of the cut rope. He plunged through a snow bridge, then into a deep crevasse. He felt sure he was about to die. Amazingly, he survived the fall. But now it seemed likely that he would freeze to death, trapped, lost, and alone in the dark crevasse.

In the morning, Simon shouted for Joe but heard nothing. Sure that Joe was dead, Simon headed back to camp. Exhausted and sad, he struggled to save himself.

Meanwhile, Joe, with a broken leg, looked for a way out of the crevasse. Amazingly, he found it. He lowered himself 80 feet (24 meters) deeper into the crevasse. There he could see a bright shaft of sunlight entering from one side. It took him six hours to crawl inch by inch up a steep 130-foot-long (40-meter-long) snow ramp. There he popped his head out through an opening to the outside world.

Joe Simpson crawled into the sunlight and down across the snowfield. It took him another three days of dragging himself along to get down the glacier, through a boulder field, to reach base camp. He did it without food and almost no water. The last, usually ten-minute walk to camp took him more than six hours. Nearing the camp at night, he called out. But he didn't know if his friend Simon was still there. But Simon was still there, and he heard Joe's weak shout.

In his thrilling book that tells this story, called

Be Prepared: The 10 Outdoor Essentials

One reason Joe Simpson survived is that he had the right equipment. Backcountry trips require that you at least bring the Ten Essentials, though much more gear is needed when doing technical climbing. Always carry:

- Map or guidebook
- Compass
- Flashlight or headlamp
- Extra food and water
- Extra clothing and raingear
- UV (ultraviolet) blocking sunglasses
- First aid kit
- Pocketknife
- Matches in a waterproof container
- Fire starter (a small bundle of paper, bark, and twigs in a waterproof container)

Touching the Void, Joe recalls that incredible moment:

"It'll be okay. I've got you. I have you; you're safe..." cried Simon Yates, who looked at his battered friend as if Joe had risen from the dead.

Joe, feeling grateful, responded, "Thanks, Simon. You did right [cutting the rope]." His friend looked away, maybe ashamed. "Anyway, thanks," said Joe.

The climbers now began the long, painful return to civilization. Their journey by mule and truck took three more days. Then there were several surgeries for Joe to endure.

Joe Simpson was a man who seemingly came back from the dead. Not only that, Joe didn't lose his leg. He recovered his strength to climb again, and to have more close brushes with death. After seeing many friends die in climbing accidents, he retired from climbing in 2003.

In 2007, Simpson said of mountaineering: "[W]hat you stand to lose far exceeds anything you stand to win. That's... climbing. You could lose your life. What do you win? A transient moment on a summit."

Chapter 5

Returning from the Dead: Beck Weathers on Everest

Mount Everest is the highest mountain on Earth. It is 29,035 feet (8,850 meters) tall. It is also the summit that many climbers dream of climbing. The people of Nepal call the peak *Chomolungma*. This means, "Mother of the Universe." But Everest is no gentle mother. It is a very dangerous place.

The first climbers to attempt Everest were Americans George Mallory and Andrew Irvine. They both died on their 1924 climb. Since then, more than two hundred climbers have died on the peak. Most of their bodies remain frozen on the mountain. It is far too risky to carry corpses down for burial.

Everest is known for its Death Zone. This area above 26,246 feet (8,000 meters) has a third less oxygen than at sea level. That makes it very hard to breathe, especially when climbing. The lack of oxygen can cause fatigue and death. Extreme cold, ice, and the chance of an avalanche add to the danger. Sudden storms with winds topping 120 miles per hour make the Death Zone very deadly.

Everest was not scaled until 1953. That's when Sir Edmund Hillary of New Zealand, and Tenzing Norgay, a Sherpa mountain guide from Nepal, reached the top and safely descended.

May 10, 1996: Disaster on Everest

By the mid-1990s many guide services were leading regular trips to Everest. Dozens of climbers tried to summit the peak each year.

Some mountaineers argue that as the number of climbers grew, safety got lax. They feel that people who weren't fit to climb could simply pay sixty thousand dollars and join an Everest expedition. They point to a single terrible day on Everest to prove their case.

On May 10, 1996, a surprise blizzard hammered several Everest expeditions. Nine climbers died that day, including two expert leaders. One of them, Rob Hall, bid his wife good-bye by cell phone from near the mountain's summit, where he froze to death.

Dr. Seaborn Beck Weathers was one of the lucky ones. Though he didn't make it quite to the top, he survived the most deadliest day in Everest's history.

Weathers was already having big problems before the blizzard struck. He went partly blind at 27,500 feet (8,382 meters), inside the Death Zone. His expedition leader, Rob Hall, ordered Weathers to stay put until Hall could summit with the rest of the climbing party. Hall promised he would then return to guide Weathers down. The trouble was, Hall never returned.

As night neared on Everest, Weathers stopped waiting for Rob Hall. He joined some other climbers heading down the mountain. They hoped to reach Camp Four, also called High Camp, at 26,000 feet (7,925 meters). Then the blizzard hit. One climber said the snow flew so thick that it was like being lost in a bottle of milk.

Weathers and the others couldn't find their way. Then the wind swept one of Beck's gloves away. His hand froze. Some climbers went on ahead to try and find High Camp. Weathers and four other exhausted climbers settled into the snow to wait for help. They fought sleep, which would mean almost certain death.

Alerted at High Camp, Russian mountaineer

Anatoli Boukreev climbed in the dark. He guided three of the five stranded climbers back to High Camp. But Boukreev was told that Weathers and famed Japanese woman climber Yasuko Namba were dead. So they were left exposed all night to the blizzard.

Rescuers arrived the next morning from High Camp. They found Weathers and Namba lying in the snow, but again left them for dead. Namba died a short time later. The rescuers radioed news of Beck Weathers's death to his wife in Dallas, Texas.

Coming Back to Life

Beck Weathers lay in the open on Mount Everest for eighteen hours in subzero weather. He should have died. But suddenly, as he lay in a hypothermic coma, near death, he awoke.

Just as suddenly, Weathers found a reason to live: "My family appeared in my mind's eye—[my wife] Peach, [my son] Bub and [daughter] Meg.... My subconscious summoned them into vivid focus, as if they might at any moment speak to me. I knew at that instant, with absolute clarity, that if I did not stand at once, I would [die at that spot]." That is what Weathers later wrote in his book *Left for Dead: My Journey Home from Everest*.

Exhausted, nearly blind, with frozen hands and face, Beck Weathers stood up. He lurched down to High Camp alone. There, fellow climbers greeted him with wonder.

Still, Beck Weathers was not safe. He was high on Everest, and in very rough shape. Everyone at High Camp felt sure that Beck wouldn't survive through the next night. After dark, another powerful gale hit. Temperatures fell. Winds roared as Weathers shivered alone in a tent. But the next morning he was not dead. Instead, he won the fight to stay alive.

Getting Back Home

Beck Weathers's rescue from Everest took almost superhuman effort, not only by Weathers, himself. It also called for caring teamwork by fellow climbers; his wife, Peach; and a daring Nepali helicopter pilot.

His rescue began when several exhausted climbers guided Beck down from High Camp to Camp Three, at 23,400 feet (7,132 meters).

Then expert mountaineer David Breashears and his expedition met Weathers. They helped him down to Camp Two at 21,300 feet (6,492 meters).

At the same time, Weathers's wife, Peach, worked nonstop to get a Nepali military helicopter to fly Beck

Altitude Sickness

Altitudes above ten thousand feet can be deadly. Climbing high means less oxygen going to the blood and to the body's tissues and cells. Too little oxygen can lead to fatigue, unconsciousness, and death. Take these tips:

- **Get used to the altitude:**
  If newly arrived in an alpine area, let your body adjust for a few days before trying to climb.
- **Climb slowly:**
  Don't gain too much altitude in one day's climb.
- **Drink water often:**
  Keeping hydrated helps avoid altitude sickness.
- **Know the symptoms:**
  Altitude sickness signs are headache, nausea, dizziness, uneven heartbeat, and shortness of breath.
- **Take action:**
  If you think you have altitude sickness, stop climbing. Go down right away.
- **Climb with a buddy:**
  Always tell that person how you're feeling. Never be afraid to give up your plans and head down.

off Everest. This was to be a very risky mission. No one had ever flown and landed this type of helicopter so high before.

Lieutenant Colonel Madan K.C., a brave Nepali pilot, flew beyond the altitude limit of his frail craft. He risked high winds that could have easily caused a crash. He rescued Weathers and another climber at 21,000 feet (6,401 meters).

Weathers's story didn't end there. Severe frostbite caused him to lose his right hand and part of his left hand. His face, too, had been terribly frostbitten and needed rebuilding. It took eleven operations for him to recover from his ordeal on Everest.

Beck Weathers learned deep life lessons from his suffering. His near-death experience made him understand how selfish and self-centered he had been when he left his family behind and went off to climb the world's tallest mountains. Now he realized that the joy and thrill in life that he had sought in high places could be found much closer to home, in day-to-day activities with his own loving family.

Words to Survive By

alpine—Relating to high mountains.

amputee—Someone who has a hand, arm, foot, leg, toe, or finger surgically removed.

avalanche—A large slide of snow and ice (or mud and rock) down a mountain.

B-24 Liberator—A World War II–era bomber plane.

belay—The securing of a rope to a mountain, down which the climber can then descend.

crevasse—A deep gap in a glacier or ice field.

delirious—Wandering of mind, lightheadedness, acting wild or crazy.

emphysema—A disease of the lungs caused by smoking, which results in serious breathing problems

fuselage—The main body of an airplane, from the cockpit back to the tail.

gangrene—The death of body tissue caused by a lack of blood supply to the tissue (sometimes the result of frostbite), which then leads to deadly bacterial infection.

parka—A heavy winter jacket.

piton—A metal spike fitted at one end with an eye for securing a rope and driven into rock or ice as a support in mountain climbing

pneumonia—A disease that inflames the lungs. It is caused by bacteria or virus.

self-arrest—A maneuver used by a mountaineer tumbling down a snow slope in which he or she rolls onto the stomach and slams an ice ax into the surrounding snow and ice as a brake to stop the fall.

Sherpa—A member of a traditional Buddhist people of Tibetan descent who lives on the south side of the Himalayas in Nepal and Sikkim. In modern times Sherpas have achieved world fame as expert guides on Himalayan mountaineering expeditions, especially on Mount Everest.

steam-powered rotary snowplow—A large, powerful spinning fan, with very sharp blades, fitted to a railroad car used to chop ice and remove snow from railroad tracks in the early 1900s.

winch—A powerful machine with a strong rope or metal cable, used for hauling or pulling.

Find Out More

Books

Anderson, Jameson. *Mountain Rescue Team.* Chicago: Raintree, 2006.

Bishop, Amanda, and Vanessa Walker. *Avalanche and Landslide Alert!* New York: Crabtree Pub., 2005.

Kyi, Tanya Lloyd. *Rescues! Ten Dramatic Stories of Life-Saving Heroics.* Toronto, Ont.: Annick Press, 2006.

Markle, Sandra. *Rescues!* Minneapolis, Minn.: Millbrook Press, 2006.

Salkeld, Audrey. *Climbing Everest: Tales of Triumph and Tragedy on the World's Highest Mountain.* Washington, D.C.: National Geographic, 2003.

Web Sites

The official site of the WestWide Avalanche Network

<http://www.avalanche.org>

MRA—the official site of the Mountain Rescue Association

<www.mra.org>

United States Search and Rescue Task Force: Avalanches

<http://www.ussartf.org/avalanches.htm>

The Mountaineers

<http://www.mountaineers.org>

Index

Read Each Title in **True Rescue Stories**

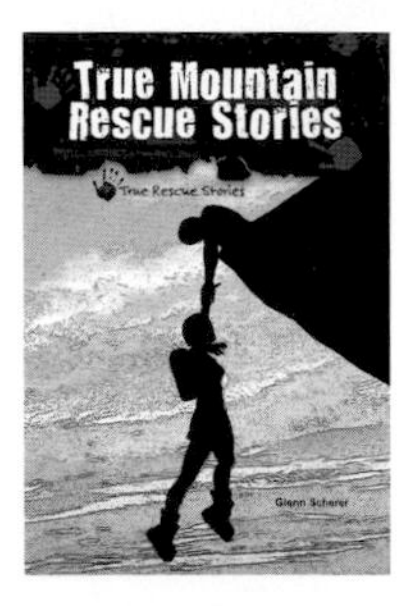

TRUE MOUNTAIN RESCUE STORIES

Shocking and triumphant true accounts of railroad wrecks, plane and helicopter crashes, and mountaineers who nearly met their maker are featured in this collection.

ISBN: 978-0-7660-3572-7

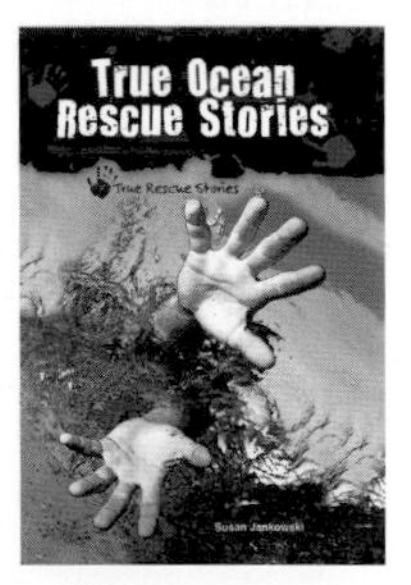

TRUE OCEAN RESCUE STORIES

A naval ship lost in battle, a vessel wrecked by an iceberg, and even a surfer rescued by a family of dolphins are some of the exciting tales of struggle and survival that will keep you on the edge of your seat.

ISBN: 978-0-7760-3665-9

TRUE UNDERGROUND RESCUE STORIES

The harrowing tales of a baby trapped in a well, a man looking for caves in Kentucky, coal miners and gold miners put in deadly predicaments, and a man rescuing another from an oncoming subway train.

ISBN: 978-0-7660-3676-5

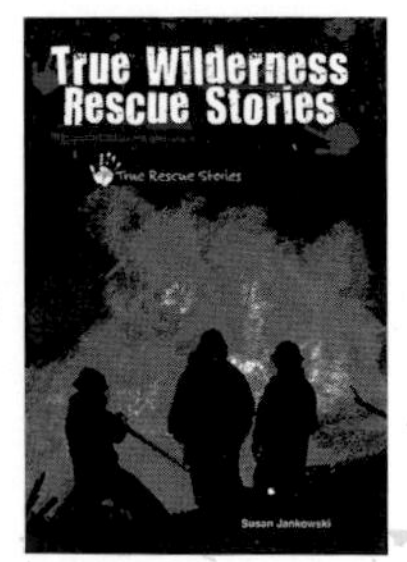

TRUE WILDERNESS RESCUE STORIES

Read about thrilling rescues that took place in the wild, such as how a person was saved from a burning forest fire, and how a group of friends was rescued by their dog.

ISBN: 978-0-7660-3666-6